CONTENTS

The state of nature in Britain. 4

Birds 8

Mammals 14

Fish 18

Amphibians and reptiles 20

Insects 22

Animals in danger 24

Help save our wildlife 28

Glossary 30

Find out more. 31

Index 32

Some words in this book appear in bold, **like this**.
You can find out what they mean by looking in the glossary.

THE STATE OF NATURE IN BRITAIN

In 2016, more than 50 organizations worked together to find out how nature and wildlife was doing throughout Britain. The State of Nature report was the result, and the news wasn't good. It said that 56 per cent of British wildlife is in **decline**. One in ten of all **species** are in danger of dying out completely. Just one species dying out can affect all the others in its **food chain**. Humans may also be affected. If insects that **pollinate** plants disappear, crops grown as food for people won't grow. This is why so many people are working hard to save our wildlife.

Impact on nature

Wildlife in Britain is affected by several problems:

Farming **Intensive farming** often involves farmers using chemicals to produce as much food as possible on their land. The use of **pesticides** affects many species. Farmers may remove certain types of habitat, such as hedges, to create larger fields. As 75 per cent of land in the UK is used for food production, this can have a huge impact on our wildlife.

G
LIFE

Success Stories

Claire Throp

raintree
a Capstone company — publishers for children

Raintree is an imprint of Capstone Global Library Limited, a company incorporated in England and Wales having its registered office at 264 Banbury Road, Oxford, OX2 7DY – Registered company number: 6695582

www.raintree.co.uk
myorders@raintree.co.uk

Edited by Helen Cox Cannons
Designed by Charmaine Whitman
Original illustrations © Capstone Global Library Limited 2018
Picture research by Jo Miller
Production by Tori Abraham
Originated by Capstone Global Library Limited
Printed and bound in India

ISBN 978 1 4747 6227 4 (hardback)
22 21 20 19 18
10 9 8 7 6 5 4 3 2 1

ISBN 978 1 4747 6229 8 (paperback)
23 22 21 20 19
10 9 8 7 6 5 4 3 2 1

British Library Cataloguing in Publication Data
A full catalogue record for this book is available from the British Library.

Acknowledgements
Alamy: Bluegreen Pictures, 19 (bottom), Margus Vilbas, 23 (top); Dreamstime: David Massaroni, 27; Getty Images: Cultura RM Exclusive/Tim E White, 5; iStockphoto: Leopardinatree, 13, SteveAllenPhoto, cover (top left); Justin Hoffmann, 1, 24, 26; Minden Pictures: David Tipling, 22; Newscom: Avalon/NHPA/Paulo de Olivelra, 19 (top); Shutterstock: D. Pimborough, 25, daseaford, 29 (bottom), Dmitry Naumov, 7, Emi, 9, Giedriius, cover (bottom), Hirundo, 29 (top), Ian Schofield, 17, IanRedding, 14, Lusine, cover (top middle), 23 (bottom), Mark Bridger, 6, Mark Medcalf, 10, 15, Martin Fowler, 21 (top), 28 (top), Rawpixel.com, 28 (bottom), Rudmer Zwerver, cover (top right), 20, Sandra Standbridge, 4, 11, Stephan Morris, 16 (top), tony mills, 8, Vector FX, 16 (bottom), 21 (bottom).
Design Elements: Shutterstock: Andrius_Saz, Bahnuz Rzayev, Davdeka, Hennadii H, Lucca Stock, Miloje, NadzeyaShanchuk.

We would like to thank Michael Bright for his invaluable help in the preparation of this book.

The animals featured on the front cover are: European otters, golden eagle, Large Blue butterfly and natterjack toad.

Every effort has been made to contact copyright holders of material reproduced in this book.
Any omissions will be rectified in subsequent printings if notice is given to the publisher.

All the internet addresses (URLs) given in this book were valid at the time of going to press. However, due to the dynamic nature of the internet, some addresses may have changed, or sites may have changed or ceased to exist since publication. While the author and publisher regret any inconvenience this may cause readers, no responsibility for any such changes can be accepted by either the author or the publisher.

Climate change **Climate change** causes temperatures and sea levels to rise, among other things. Powerful storms can damage animal and plant habitats.

People **Birds of prey**, such as eagles, are often killed as people believe they are hunting smaller animals and birds. Some birds, such as pheasants, are raised to be hunted for sport. Sometimes, people steal eggs from nests.

The shooting of birds of prey is against the law. But sadly this does not stop some people from doing it anyway.

Conservation groups

Conservation groups, such as the Royal Society for the Protection of Birds (RSPB) and the Wildlife Trusts, often work together to save species and their habitats. A lot of their work is carried out by **volunteers**. TV programmes focusing on nature, such as *Springwatch*, can help to make more people aware of the problems faced by wildlife.

harvest mouse

Conservation methods

Often a mix of different conservation methods is needed in order to help a species. One of the first things conservationists need to do is count the bird, animal, insect or plant to see whether or not it is at risk. This is easier with some species than others. Some birds can be counted in flight, but other animals, such as the harvest mouse, are very difficult to find.

Land management

Land management involves restoring habitats and creating new ones. It means planting hedges and other plants that particular animals feed on. Creating as large a habitat as possible for a variety of species allows them to thrive. The RSPB's Mersehead nature reserve in Scotland was originally in two parts. But in 2017 the RSPB were able to buy the land in-between, creating an even larger area for nature.

Reintroduction programmes

Wildlife doesn't always return to restored habitats naturally and may need some help. **Captive-bred** wild animals, or those rescued after illness or injury, can be **reintroduced** to a habitat. Sometimes, if there is a low number of a certain animal, these animals are brought in to new habitats from other countries where they are thriving.

Reintroduction programmes only go ahead if certain conditions are met. Conservationists have to think about a number of questions. Will that particular species be able to thrive in the habitat? Is it a place where the species once lived? What effect might the reintroduction have on other species in that habitat?

Charities, conservationists and volunteers have been working hard to help save species from **extinction** in Britain. This book looks at some of those success stories.

Using binoculars allows you to see wild birds and animals clearly, but from a distance so that you don't disturb them.

BIRDS

Over 600 bird species live in Britain all year round. Many more **breed** here, spend the winter here or travel through on their way to somewhere else. Some birds that were close to extinction or even extinct in Britain have been brought back by some clever conservation work.

This is a starling murmuration. Thousands of starlings whirl around the sky together before landing to roost. This group of starlings were at the RSPB Marazion Marsh reserve in Cornwall.

RED KITES

Red kites are birds of prey. By the 1870s, they were extinct in all parts of Britain except Wales. Chemicals in the birds' food chain and **persecution** by humans, including people collecting eggs from the birds' nests, had wiped them out. The government passed laws to give special protection to the birds. But kites are slow breeders, so conservationists decided that they needed extra help.

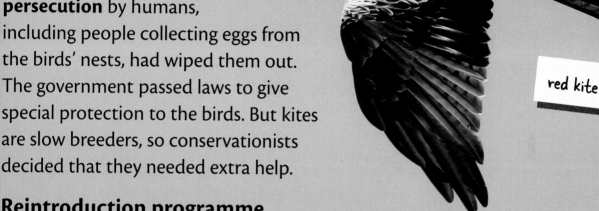

red kite

Reintroduction programme

In 1989, the RSPB, Natural England and Scottish Natural Heritage started a programme of reintroduction. This involved bringing red kites from Wales and Spain to England and Scotland. The first two sites were in Buckinghamshire, in southern England, and in Ross-shire, in north Scotland. All the birds were given plastic wing tags, each of which had a code that would allow the bird to be recognized. Over the years, more birds were reintroduced to different areas of England and Scotland. Successful breeding by these birds meant that numbers gradually increased. Red kites are now a common sight in the skies over many parts of Britain.

Red kite

Lives: central Wales; Buckinghamshire/ Oxfordshire area, Northamptonshire, Yorkshire, Gateshead and Grizedale Forest in Cumbria; Dumfries and Galloway, Stirlingshire and west Perthshire, around Black Isle in Ross-shire, Aberdeen City

Habitats: woodland, **grassland**, farmland

Eats: dead animals, worms, small mammals

Success story:

1903: "several breeding pairs" 🐦
present: 1,600–1,800 breeding pairs

🐦🐦🐦🐦🐦🐦🐦🐦🐦
🐦🐦🐦🐦🐦🐦🐦🐦

🐦 = 100 breeding pairs

WHITE-TAILED EAGLES

Like other birds of prey, white-tailed eagles were persecuted by people during the 1800s. This was because the eagles fed on animals and birds that people wanted to hunt. The last British white-tailed eagle was shot in Scotland in 1916. In 1975, conservation groups brought eagles from Norway to the island of Rum in the Western Isles of Scotland, as part of a reintroduction programme. Laws to protect birds of prey were also created.

White-tailed eagles do not begin to breed until they are 4 or 5 years old, so numbers were slow to increase. RSPB Scotland **monitored** and protected any new nesting sites. Finally, in 2015, volunteers counted 100 breeding pairs. It is thought that the eagle **population** will now be able to continue growing without the need for any more reintroduction projects.

white-tailed eagle

CIRL BUNTINGS

Cirl buntings were once common, particularly in the south of England. But by the late 1980s, they were rare. The RSPB investigated and found that changes in farming practices had caused the bird's numbers to fall. Farmers were using more pesticides, chopping down hedges to create larger fields and planting crops in autumn rather than spring. This meant there were fewer insects and seeds for cirl buntings and their young to eat. Loss of hedgerows resulted in fewer places for the birds to nest.

The RSPB worked with wildlife-friendly farmers in Devon, encouraging them to plant grassy areas around fields and to sow barley in the spring. The fields were then left as **stubble** for the cirl buntings to feed on. The RSPB's plan aimed for 1,000 breeding pairs of cirl buntings by 2020. In 2016, 1,079 pairs were recorded – an increase of more than 800 per cent!

cirl bunting

Cirl bunting

Lives: Devon, Cornwall

Habitats: farmland, grassland

Eats: insects, seeds

Success story:

1989: 120 breeding pairs 🐦 🐦

present: 1,079 breeding pairs

🐦🐦🐦🐦🐦
🐦🐦🐦🐦🐦

🐦 = 100 breeding pairs

BITTERNS

Bitterns were extinct in Britain by the late 1800s. People hunted them for food, and the birds' **reedbed** habitat had all but disappeared. Reedbeds can dry out, particularly if other plants are allowed to take over. In normal circumstances, new reedbeds would emerge. But the number of house-building and construction projects in Britain over the years has prevented new natural reedbeds developing. Bittern numbers began to rise again from 1911, but by 1997, numbers had fallen once more – only 11 males were recorded in that year.

Research on bitterns

The RSPB carried out research and developed plans to save the bittern. One of the first things conservationists needed to do was restore and manage reedbeds, and create new ones. This involved keeping water levels high, creating open water areas and introducing fish to those areas for the bitterns to eat. Linking the reedbeds helped to create a larger habitat for bitterns to feed and breed in.

Climate change and rising sea levels are still dangers for these birds, but numbers are increasing. There were 162 males recorded in 2016/2017.

Bittern

Lives: southern England, East Anglia, Lancashire

Habitat: reedbeds

Eats: fish, amphibians, invertebrates

Success story:

1997: 11 males

2016: 162 males

= 10 birds

bittern

Counting bitterns

It is difficult to count bitterns because they are very secretive. Their colouring allows them to hide easily among the reeds. Conservationists count bitterns by recording the male bird's booming call. Each bittern's call is different, so scientists can listen to the calls on a computer and work out how many individual birds there are.

MAMMALS

There are 101 species of mammals living in Britain and in the seas around the country. Most are native to Britain but some have been introduced from another country, such as the grey squirrel, which came from North America in the 1870s. These introduced species have often caused problems for our native mammals.

GREATER HORSESHOE BATS

A loss of places for greater horseshoe bats to roost and hibernate has led to a fall in numbers over the last 100 years. Their main food source of insects has been affected by changes in farming practices and the use of more pesticides. To help the bats, conservation groups have set up roosting reserves for them. They also monitor and improve roosting sites, and investigate the use of pesticides on insects. Gradually, greater horseshoe bats are increasing in numbers, although they are still much lower than in 1900.

Greater horseshoe bat

Lives: south-west England, Sussex, south, north and west Wales

Habitats: old buildings, caves, old mines

Eats: beetles, moths, crane flies

Success story: = 1,000 bats

1900: 300,000

2005: 6,600

2016: 10,000

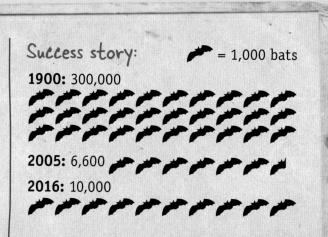

OTTERS

Otters were nearly wiped out in England during the 1950s and 1960s. This was due to pesticides washing into and poisoning the rivers where otters live. Otters were also once hunted by people. In 1978, they were made a protected species, which means it is against the law to harm them.

Otter numbers are now increasing, thanks to the cleaning up of rivers and waterways, the banning of harmful pesticides and conservation projects to provide new habitats. In some areas, such as East Anglia, reintroductions also took place in the 1980s. In 2011, it was announced that otters have now returned to every county in England.

Counting otters

Counting otters is hard to do because they travel quite long distances and are very secretive. They are also nocturnal, which means they are active at night. Instead of counting, researchers look for evidence of otters. This evidence includes footprints and spraints – otherwise known as otter poo!

Otter

Lives: throughout Britain

Habitats: rivers, ditches, **fens**, reedbeds

Eats: fish, amphibians, small mammals and birds

Success story:

1977–1979:
Otters found at 5.8% of sites visited

2010:
Otters found at 58.8% of sites visited

POLECATS

Polecats were once common in Britain but their numbers fell during the 1800s. Loss of the polecat's woodland habitat led to the species becoming extremely rare in England and Wales. They were killed by **gamekeepers** to stop them taking birds that people wanted to hunt. Polecats also got caught in traps meant for other animals. By 1915, central Wales was the only place left in Britain where polecats could be found.

Gradually, polecat numbers began to rise again due to less persecution. From 1993, the Vincent Wildlife Trust began to research polecats and they have since done three national polecat surveys. They are also doing research on threats to polecat numbers. Many polecats are killed on roads. Some die from eating rats that have been poisoned. Rats are a natural source of food for polecats.

Polecats are now found in areas of Britain where they have not been seen for many years. Conservationists believe polecats will continue to grow in numbers.

Polecat

Lives: Wales, most of England, particularly the south and west

Habitats: woodland, hedgerows, farmland

Eats: wild rabbits, rats, small birds, frogs, toads, worms

Success story: ■ = polecat range

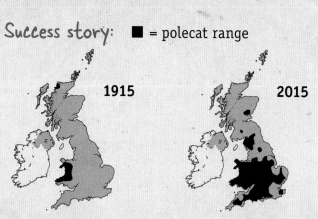

1915

2015

WATER VOLES

Water voles are the largest species of vole in Britain. Their numbers fell throughout the 1900s because of changes in farming practices, which led to a loss of habitat. Since the late 1970s, their numbers have **declined** by 90 per cent. The other main problem faced by water voles is an introduced species of mammal called the American mink. They were originally brought to Britain in the 1930s for their fur, but some escaped or were released into the countryside. American minks are predators and have been responsible for killing many water voles.

The Wildlife Trusts have set up projects to help water voles. The projects involve improving river habitats and trying to control numbers of American minks. The Trusts have worked with other organizations and local landowners. In 2011, a reintroduction programme at Rutland Water was successful. It means that water voles now exist in every English county, although some of these are only very small populations.

FISH

There are about 330 species of fish living in the seas around Britain, including well-known species such as cod and plaice.

ATLANTIC COD

Cod stocks in the North Sea peaked at 270,000 tonnes in the 1970s, but fell to just 44,000 tonnes in 2006. Cod have been over-fished for many years. The fishermen wanted to catch cod for people to eat but over time they have caught too many young cod. These cod were not old enough to breed so numbers fell drastically.

Cod Recovery Plan

The fishing industry worked with the Scottish government and the European Union Fisheries Council to put in place a Cod Recovery Plan. The aim was to reduce the amount of cod caught by fishing boats by 25 per cent in 2009. Each year after that, there was to be another 10 per cent reduction. New types of net for catching the fish were tried out. Areas of the coast where the females laid their eggs were set aside as safe areas where no fishing was allowed. Boats were checked to see that the fishermen had kept their catches of fish to a reasonable level.

Cod

Lives: in the sea all around Britain (and Scandinavia)

Habitat: sea (colder water)

Eats: worms, prawns, crabs, octopus, smaller fish such as sandeels

Success story: ➤ = 10,000 tonnes

1970s: 270,000 tonnes

2006: 44,000 tonnes

2015: 149,000 tonnes

These measures have led to a growth in numbers of Atlantic cod. In July 2017, the Marine Stewardship Council (MSC) said that cod was once again **sustainable**. While this means that the MSC think Atlantic cod is safe from extinction, numbers are still much lower than they were 50 years ago.

MSC blue label

Fish that are considered sustainable by the Marine Stewardship Council are sold in shops with a blue label attached. The fisheries they come from have been investigated to see what impact they have on fish populations and their food chains. The MSC blue label is only given if a fishery meets very strict guidelines.

Cod fishing boat on the North Sea

AMPHIBIANS AND REPTILES

There are six reptile species and seven species of amphibian living in Britain.

NATTERJACK TOADS

Natterjack toads are very rare in Britain. Loss of the toad's coastal habitat led to a fall in numbers. Now reintroduction programmes are helping. In 2013, the RSPB restored sand **dunes** destroyed by storms at their nature reserve at Mersehead, Scotland. Thirty male toads were counted at the start of the project, but this number had increased to 150 by 2016.

Counting natterjack toads

Male natterjack toads are counted by listening out for their very loud call to find where they are. Photographs are then taken so that the same toads are not counted more than once. Each toad has a unique pattern of warts and a yellow stripe on its back. Females are more difficult to count, so the number of spawn strings (jelly that contains the toad's eggs) are also counted. The two sets of figures are then added together.

SAND LIZARD

Farming and development of land for houses and roads has led to the destruction of much of the sand lizard's **heathland** habitat. Conservation groups, including the Amphibian and Reptile Conservation Trust, have worked to protect the few remaining sites. They have also recreated heathland and sand dunes for the lizards.

In the early 1990s, conservationists agreed that captive breeding of sand lizards followed by reintroduction was a good way to help save the species. As of 2012, about 9,000 sand lizards had been released through the reintroduction programme. They have been restored to seven counties where the lizard had died out. Sand lizards are now living in north Wales. They have not been seen there for 50 years.

Sand lizard

Lives: Dorset, Hampshire and Surrey, on sand dunes in Lancashire; reintroduced into areas in south-east England and Wales

Habitats: coastal sand dunes, heathlands

Eats: insects, invertebrates (such as worms and slugs)

Success story:

- ● Sand lizards recently found
- ○ Sand lizards recently reintroduced

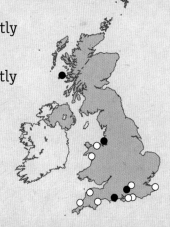

INSECTS

Britain has about 27,000 different insect species, including 59 species of butterfly.

LARGE BLUE BUTTERFLIES

The Large Blue butterfly was extinct in Britain by 1979. The reasons include habitat loss, changes in farming practices and a disease that killed many of Britain's wild rabbits. Rabbits' feeding habits help to create the perfect grassland areas for a plant called wild thyme, which Large Blues feed on.

Reintroduction of the Large Blue

In the early 1980s, a site in Dartmoor in southern England owned by the National Trust was chosen for a reintroduction programme. First of all, the land had to be managed carefully. The temperature of the ground had to be just right for red ants to thrive (see "Cunning caterpillars" box). The temperature is affected by the height of the grass. Livestock (cows and sheep) were brought in to graze the land in spring and autumn. The land had to be fenced off, with trees and **scrubland** removed. Once the red ants were doing well, conservationists brought in Large Blue butterfly eggs from Sweden. The reintroduction was successful. By 1985, Large Blues were once again living in Britain.

Large Blue butterfly showing top of wings

Larva of Large Blue butterfly with a red ant

Cunning caterpillars

In the 1970s, a scientist discovered that the caterpillars of the Large Blue butterfly trick their way into the nests of a single species of red ant. The caterpillars make noises and give off a smell that fools the ants into believing that they are grubs (young ants). They get carried into the ants' nest and then spend the next 10 months eating all the red ant grubs. While other species of red ant will take the caterpillars into their nests, they are soon recognized and killed.

Numbers of the Large Blue have continued to increase and Britain now has the largest population in the world. Habitat improvements made for the Large Blue have also allowed other insects to thrive, as well as rare plants, such as the musk orchid.

Large Blue butterfly showing underside of wings

ANIMALS IN DANGER

While there are conservation success stories, there are many other animals, birds and insects still in need of our help. You may see a lot of starlings in your area, for example, but their numbers have fallen in recent years. There are 79 per cent fewer starlings now than there were in 1979.

Red squirrels have suffered from the introduction of grey squirrels. Grey squirrels have taken over in much of Britain, pushing red squirrels back to Scotland and just a few areas in the rest of Britain. Turtle doves, nightingales and bumblebees are all facing an uncertain time as their numbers continue to fall. But they are not the only ones.

red squirrel

HEDGEHOGS

Hedgehog numbers have fallen 97 per cent – from 35 million to 1 million – since the 1950s. They are disappearing at the same rate as tigers in Asia. Habitat loss, such as fewer hedgerows and more cars on the roads, are the main reasons. People are also keeping their gardens tidier and putting up fences. This means that hedgehogs have more difficulty moving from place to place to feed.

Hedgehog Street is a campaign that began in 2011 to help hedgehogs. It's run by People's Trust for Endangered Species and the British Hedgehog Preservation Society (BHPS). The aim is to link as many gardens as possible, by making or leaving holes in-between fences or in walls. It also means making sure gardens are safe for hedgehogs and putting out healthy food for them.

V-MOTH

V-moth numbers have fallen by 99 per cent from 1968 to 2007. It is thought that our gardening habits are partly responsible. V-moth caterpillars feed on gooseberry and currant leaves, but these plants are no longer common in our gardens. Gardeners using pesticides are also bad news for moths and other insects.

ATLANTIC PUFFINS

Atlantic puffins are at risk of extinction because of sea **pollution**. Climate change is causing sea temperatures to rise, resulting in fewer of the puffin's main food – sandeels. Also, large numbers of sandeels are fished in the North Sea. This means that young puffins do not have enough to eat. Fewer birds survive to continue breeding. On Fair Isle, an island in Scotland, between the years 1986 and 2016, numbers of puffins halved (from 20,000 to 10,000).

Atlantic puffin

WHITE-CLAWED CRAYFISH

The white-clawed crayfish is Britain's only native crayfish. It was once common but now there are very few left. Pollution, habitat loss and a disease called crayfish plague have caused the fall in numbers. An introduced species, the American Signal crayfish, has also affected their numbers. Ark sites have been set up to help. Ark sites are protected places, away from other species of crayfish, including those that might carry diseases.

Nature needs you!

It is fantastic that some animals and birds have been saved by conservationists and are now thriving. But we must make sure that other species are rescued too. And you can help! See the tips on the next page for some ideas about how to get started.

HELP SAVE OUR WILDLIFE

There are many things you and your family and friends can do to help conserve and encourage the wildlife around you.

Top tips for saving wildlife

1. Join a wildlife conservation group. The RSPB, the Wildfowl & Wetlands Trust, the Wildlife Trusts – these are just a few of the conservation groups that you can join in Britain.

2. Give up some of your pocket money! Giving money to conservation groups helps them to pay for all the things they need to do to help wildlife.

3. Volunteer! Jobs such as hedge-laying or tree-planting are often done by people who offer their time and skills for free. Get your family involved too!

4. You could also visit an outdoor education centre. You can try nature activities and learn more about wildlife.

5. If you have a garden, make sure it is as wildlife-friendly as possible. You could ask adults to avoid using plastic netting because animals can get caught in it. You could also ask them to avoid using chemical weedkillers. They can harm wildlife as well as killing weeds.

6. Leave some areas of your garden messy and plant flowers that will attract insects. Include bird feeders and water, and make sure you clean the feeders regularly. If you think you have other animal visitors, such as hedgehogs, place food and water out for them too. Just don't leave them bread and milk. These make hedgehogs very sick.

dome–shaped shelter for a hedgehog

shelter for wild animals and insects

7. If you don't have a garden, there are other things you can do, such as create a small pond from a washing-up bowl. Ask an adult to help you find somewhere to hang bird feeders. You can even buy feeders that stick on the window, so you can see birds up-close.

8. Tell other people! Make sure everyone knows how amazing wildlife is and how many of our species are at risk from extinction. Keeping the natural world in balance is important for humans too. We can all do our bit to help nature in Britain.

GLOSSARY

breed mate and produce young

captive breeding breeding wild animals in places such as zoos and safari parks. It is used when a species has become very rare, ensuring that it does not die out completely.

climate change significant change in Earth's climate over a period of time

conservation protection of animals and plants, as well as the wise use of what humans get from nature

decline fall; go down

dune hill or ridge of sand piled up by the wind

extinct no longer living; an extinct animal is one that has died out, with no more of its kind

fen flat, marshy land that is often flooded

food chain series of living things that are linked to each other. Each creature feeds on the next one in the chain.

gamekeeper person who manages the wild animals and birds kept on someone's land for the purpose of hunting

grassland large area of wild grasses

heathland open area of land covered in grasses with few trees

intensive farming type of farming that aims to produce as much food as possible, often using chemicals

monitor check regularly

persecution cruel treatment

pesticide poisonous chemical used to kill insects, rats and other pests that can damage plants

pollinate when an insect, bird or the wind carries pollen between flowering plants, which means the plants can make seeds to create new plants

pollution harmful materials that damage the air, water and soil

population group of animals or plants living in a certain place

reedbed area of water or marshland that has mostly reeds in it

reintroduce bring back an animal or plant to an area where it was once common but from which it had disappeared

scrubland land with low bushes and grasses

species group of animals with similar features

stubble cut stalks of cereal plants left in the ground after the grain is harvested

sustainable able to be kept at a certain or reasonable level

volunteer person who does something because they want to help, not because they are paid

FIND OUT MORE

Books

British Wildlife, Camilla de la Bedoyere (Miles Kelly, 2014)

Climate Change (Question It!), Philip Steele (Wayland, 2017)

Habitats (Moving Up With Science), Peter Riley (Franklin Watts, 2016)

Natural Habitats (Question It!), Philip Steele (Wayland, 2017)

Websites

www.bats.org.uk/pages/batsforkids.html
Go to the Bat Conservation Trust's website to learn more about bats in the UK and what you can do to help them.

www.hedgehogstreet.org
Learn how to help hedgehogs!

www.wildlifewatch.org.uk/activity-sheets
Try some of these fun ideas to help you find out more about wildlife. You can make a butterfly feeder, a nest box or even a wildlife pond.

ypte.org.uk/audiences/kids
The Young People's Trust for the Environment has information about the effect that humans have on animals' habitats and how we can look after the world.

Conservation groups

There are many conservation groups in the UK. There are national groups such as the RSPB, which protects birds and animals in Britain and abroad. Others, such as the Wildlife Trusts, have many local groups. There are also organizations that focus on protecting one type of wildlife. The Bat Conservation Trust, the British Dragonfly Society, Butterfly Conservation, the Marine Conservation Society … if there is a type of animal or insect that you are interested in, you are bound to be able to find a group that wants to protect it. Ask an adult to help you find out more by looking online.

INDEX

amphibians and reptiles 20–21

birds 8–13, 24, 26, 29
birds of prey 5, 9–10
bitterns 12–13
bumblebees 24
butterflies and moths 22–23, 26

captive breeding 7, 21
caterpillars 23, 26
chemicals 4, 9, 11, 14, 15, 16, 26, 28
cirl buntings 11
climate change 5, 12, 26
cod, Atlantic 18–19
conservation groups, supporting 28
conservation methods 6–7
counts and surveys 6, 11, 13, 15, 16, 20
crayfish 27

egg theft 5, 9
endangered species 4, 24–27

farming 4, 11, 14, 17, 22
fish 18–19
food chains 4, 9, 19

gamekeepers 16
gardens 25, 26, 28–29
greater horseshoe bats 14

habitats and habitat loss 4, 6, 7, 12, 15, 16,
    17, 20, 21, 22, 23, 25, 27
harvest mice 6
hedgehogs 25, 29

insects 4, 14, 22–23, 24, 26, 29
introduced species 14, 17, 24, 27

land management 6, 12, 22

mammals 14–17
minks 17

natterjack toads 20
nature reserves 6, 8, 20
nightingales 24

orchids 23
otters 15
overfishing 18

persecution 4, 5, 9, 10, 12, 15, 16
pesticides 4, 11, 14, 15, 26
polecats 16
pollution 26, 27
protected species 9, 15
puffins 26

rabbits 22
red and grey squirrels 14, 24
red kites 9
reintroduction programmes 7, 9, 10, 17, 20,
    21, 22

sand lizards 21
saving wildlife, ideas for 28–29
starlings 8, 24
State of Nature report (2016) 4

traps 16
turtle doves 24

volunteers 5, 7, 10, 28

water voles 17
white-tailed eagles 10